Ta~~king N~~

Fr~~~~

A G~~uide~~ for Students

Sandra Ashman and Phyllis Creme

University of North London

Taking Notes From Lectures

Sandra Ashman & Phyllis Creme

First published 1980

by the University of North London Press

2nd revised edition 1990

3rd edition 1993

This edition 1996

ISBN 1 85377 017 5

University of North London

166-220 Holloway Road, London N7 8DB

© 1996

The University of North London is a Charity and a Company
Limited by Guarantee.
Registered in England No. 1000834.

Contents

1
From Lessons to Lectures

When you first start your course, you will be meeting a particular kind of routine which will be rather different from school, college, work or home. Depending on what you are studying, your time will be divided between lectures, smaller group seminars, perhaps tutorials, and, if you are on a science course, practicals.

On many courses, you will have more free time for independent study than you will have had previously. And, whatever your course, a large part of your timetabled work will involve listening to lectures. In this booklet, we will discuss learning from lectures, and in particular, taking notes from them.

Let's think first about some of the differences between lectures in higher education and those on your A-level course. For instance, the subjects you learned at A-level - for example, history or biology, are now broken down into more specialised subject areas - the nineteenth century, or economic history; population biology and metabolism. Broadly speaking, each new subject area will have a different lecturer, each with a different lecturing style and approach to the subject. If there are links to be made between subject areas, it will often be up to you to make them, because the lecturers tend to be used to thinking according to their own discipline. In many cases, they will be carrying out research into their subject at a highly specialised level. Listening to a lecture is sometimes rather like being taken into a foreign country with its own language and ways of thinking. This can be exciting, but can also cause difficulties, until you become familiar with the terminology and concepts. It is generally considered that by the time you reach higher education, the responsibility for your learning in the institution you attend is yours, not your lecturer's. Of course, you can expect various kinds of help from your lecturers and tutors, but it is you who has to take the initiative in your learning. We hope that you will find this booklet useful in tackling one aspect of your study.

2
Why Take Notes?

Making notes, whether from your reading or from lectures, is the means by which you build up a personal record of your learning on the whole of your course. The act of taking notes also helps you to learn as you go along. So, to decide why notes are so essential, we need to consider these two points: first, how does taking notes help you to learn more effectively, and secondly, what are you going to use the notes for later on?

How does taking notes help learning?

Note-taking encourages active learning. Whenever you listen to a lecture, read a book, or take part in a seminar you are processing the information you receive. The ideas you are able to take in and absorb depend on how much you understand, how they relate to what you already know, and on your sense of what you need the information for. Your notes are therefore a running commentary of your own particular interpretation of what you hear or read. The very act of taking notes helps you to process the information effectively, to concentrate, to keep alert and to think. Research shows that taking notes at the time also helps you to remember the material later on.

What will you use your notes for?

Probably the main use of notes will be as a *'memory aid'* later on when you are revising for exams. You may also use them as material for an essay or seminar paper. Sometimes, you will have a clear idea of what you will use your notes for as you take them, but in other cases, you may not. So you could at this stage consider why you yourself take notes; you may have other reasons other than those we have given. You could also consider how far the notes you have taken lately are effective for your particular purposes. Are they a good memory aid? Can you understand them? In general, how usable are they? It is often very easy to take down a mass of notes, almost mechanically, sometimes in panic, and to feel better. Often, however, when you come to look back at these notes, you will find that your sense of security was ill-founded and you can't make much sense of them. Our suggestions for note-taking should help you, but first let's consider some general aspects of learning from lectures.

3
Learning from Lectures

What does a lecture do?

It is important to remember the differences between learning from lectures and from books. The most obvious difference is that, in a lecture, you have to start at the beginning and end where the lecturer finishes; you can't backtrack. You also have to go at the lecturer's pace, with no scope for slowing down or speeding up according to your own level of understanding or state of attentiveness. On the other hand, this disadvantage can be offset by the fact that the lecturer is a real person who can be asked questions. What is more, since lecturers know more about the particular needs of the course than any book, they can process a wide range of information and make it relevant to your syllabus and level of knowledge. In other words, lectures can save you a good deal of time.

It is interesting and useful to think about what lectures are doing. We have just suggested that they may be presenting you with some pre-digested information. But what kind of information? This will vary widely according to the subject as well as the lecture. You may be hearing an explanation or interpretation of the meaning of the facts - the lecturer's own viewpoint, or several different interpretations for you to consider. You may be hearing an account of a logical process, a calculation, or explanation of a theory, or the lecturer may be concerned with causes and effects. Lecturers are doing many different things and if you have some overview of what kind of lecture you are listening to, you will find it much easier to understand and take notes from it. We deal with this in more detail later on.

Closely related to what a lecture is doing is its shape or structure. It is sometimes possible to express this graphically - below are some examples. Trying to formulate the structure in this way can be an interesting and very useful exercise.

The structure of lectures
Example 1

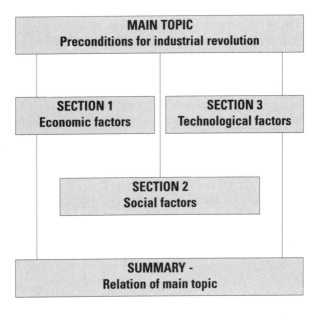

In this example, the main topic is introduced and then dealt with in three subsections - the economic, social and technological factors. Finally these three are brought together and summed up in relationship to the main topic.

Example 2
How to design a printed circuit board

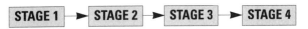

This shows how a lecture can be approached in a linear fashion, dealing stage by stage with the design of a circuit board.

Example 3
Characteristics of Wordsworth's poetry

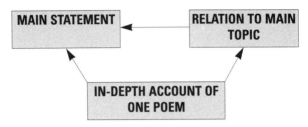

Here the lecturer deals with the characteristics of Wordsworth's poems by presenting these through a detailed analysis of one poem, returning then to a more general overview of the subject.

When you are taking notes in lectures, try to pick up as many clues as possible, either beforehand or early on in the lecture, about the structure that the lecturer intends to use. This will help you to get a clearer picture of the material presented, both in your mind and on your page of notes.

4
The Three Stages

Stage 1: Before the lecture
There are a number of ways in which you can focus on a lecture beforehand, to help you learn from it.

i The title and the syllabus
Is the lecture part of a written-out syllabus? Usually, you will have been given a course programme with titles of lectures and perhaps notes about them (if you have not been given a written programme, you could ask the lecturer for one). If you know the title, think about, or preferably discuss with a friend, what the title might mean and the kinds of questions it raises for you. Try to relate this particular lecture to the rest of the syllabus. How does it seem to fit in to the whole picture? In particular, look back at last week's notes to jog your memory.

ii Advance reading
The course programme will include suggested readings, sometimes for each individual lecture. The point of advance preparation is to orientate you to the subject of the lecture. Don't imagine that any advance reading you do might make attending the lecture a waste of time. The lecturer may reinforce ideas from your reading, but will more likely raise questions about it or deal with a particular aspect in depth. It will certainly help the lecturer's job if s/he can assume knowledge on the part of the students, and this is why suggestions for advance reading are given.

iii Don't be late!
It is an obvious point, but nevertheless important, that you need to arrive on time for the lecture. Give yourself time to settle down where you can

hear and see the lecturer and to find your paper and pen. If you rush in five minutes late, with no idea of what it's all supposed to be about, you might spend the next half hour trying to find out.

Stage 2: During the lecture
Here we want to stress the importance of active listening and selection and this includes looking for 'signposts' and 'key words'.

i Active listening
In all these study guides, we emphasise that you have to do your own learning - it can't be done for you. It can sometimes be difficult to remember this when you are sitting in a lecture listening to someone else speak: but it is no use trying to soak in information like a sponge. Even if you could do it (and our minds don't work in this way), you would still be expected to do something with the information later on; when you write essays or exams, for instance.

The more you analyse the material as you hear it, the more likely you are to be able to apply it and relate it to what else you know. We have suggested that asking questions about the lecture beforehand can help you to listen actively. Ask yourself questions during the lecture too - what does this mean? - how does this fit in with what I've read? - do I agree? - how does he get that particular solution there? We have said, too, that the very act of taking notes helps you to listen actively since it requires you to process the information for yourself straight away.

ii Signposts
Active listening will help you to grasp the kind of lecture you are listening to - which is to do with what the lecturer is aiming to get across, and the kind of structure it has. One way of helping yourself answer this is to look for a variety of verbal 'signposts' which indicate where the lecturer is

going and what s/he is doing. The lecture will usually begin with a statement outlining the topic of the lecture.

'Today I'm going to look at...'

'I am going to discuss the three main aspects of this subject...'

(Sometimes, however, it can be difficult to make out what the 'three main aspects' are in the course of the lecture - or the lecturer may actually only discuss two and a half!).

Other 'signposts' that crop up during the lecture may indicate the beginning and end of a section:

'Let's start by looking at..'

'Now we'll go on to...'

'Now we'll leave that for the time being and move on to...'

Often lecturers will periodically sum up the points they have been making:

'So what we have here is...'

'To sum up ... in a word'

'To put it another way, what I am trying to say is...'

You can also look out for indications of what the lecturer considers important, frequently by repetition, or by such phrases as:

'We must always remember that...' or

'I want to emphasise...'

Lecturers may actually dictate notes that they think are particularly important, such as quotations.

Sometimes the 'signposts' are non-verbal. For instance, when the lecturers write on the board or use an overhead projector, it is often because you are intended to copy down the information, though it may also be because a visual aid reinforces the explanation. If they say something more slowly, or pause, it is often for emphasis (though it may also be a sign of hard thinking!). You will be able to spot different non-verbal signposts in different lecturers.

Watch out, too, for digressions.

'By the way...' or

'Well, to get back to the main point...'

Sometimes these digressions are right off the point and designed primarily to give both you and the lecturer a break; sometimes they are relevant to the subject matter in general, but if they are something that has just occurred to the lecturer, they may not fit into the outline plan he has presented to you. So digressions can be very interesting and useful as long as they don't confuse you.

Handouts are a common aid to lecturers. These serve different purposes and vary in their usefulness, depending on the lecturer. They may provide an outline of the lecture to give you an overview from the beginning. They may include some material for you to examine during the lecture, or highlight some particularly important points. Some lecturers provide a series of questions for the students to consider during the lecture. Whatever their purpose, use them - and don't leave them in the lecture room! Look at them after the lecture to reinforce its content in your memory.

Lecturers will, of course, differ in how they structure their lectures and how much, therefore, they provide you with 'signposts'. Some lecturers are more organised than others and you will have to adapt to a wide variety of styles and presentation. The main thing you are looking for is an understanding of what the lecturer's main points and general headings are, and how these points are developed and explained in the lecture. It is most important to distinguish between the important points and the details, and looking for 'signposts' will help you to do this.

iii Selection

Looking for the main points of the lecture leads us on to the question of selection in note-taking. Lecturers often complain that students try to write down everything they say. But deciding how much detail to include can be difficult. There is no standard answer to this question: you will need to work out what is best for your particular needs. As we emphasised before, you take notes for different purposes and the amount of detail you need to include will depend on what use the notes will serve.

It isn't very often appropriate to take down as much as you can possibly manage, because it only postpones the task of processing the information into a set of notes that are appropriate for your particular study needs. Whilst it is true that just occasionally you might consider that a lecture is so valuable that you want to record every word of it, this would be best achieved with a tape recorder. At the other extreme, if you know the information is easily obtainable elsewhere, then you may want only very brief notes.

Broadly speaking, though, you should aim to get down enough information, and no more, to *enable you to reconstruct the material at a later date.* For this, you need an outline of what is said, with supporting details. This involves both getting down something of what the lecturer says and also an indication of how the ideas relate to each other and which are more, and which less, important.

How do you discover what the lecturer's main ideas are? We do realise that this may not be easy and certainly it is more difficult with some lecturers than others. But if you understand the importance of questioning, of attentive listening, and of trying to relate the lecture to what you already know, you will begin to get an idea of what information you need to record for your particular study needs.

Perhaps the biggest difficulty comes when you don't fully understand the lecture, or you can't keep up with it. Unfortunately there is no simple remedy for this, but there are ways in which you can begin to tackle the problem yourself. For instance, first try to check whether the problem applies to a good proportion of the students in the class; it could be that the lecturer's approach is too advanced or that his presentation makes comprehension difficult. In this case, it is clearly something to discuss, either with the lecturer or with your tutor.

If it applies only to yourself, or to a few other students, try to work out the reasons. Is it because you haven't carried out enough advance preparation for the lecture? Is it because you have difficulty in understanding the lecturer's English? Are you too unfamiliar with the whole subject area of the lecture, so much so that you have too little background knowledge to relate the new ideas to? Again, there are no easy answers but if you try to pinpoint the reasons, you are in a better position both to seek help from others and to work on solutions for yourself.

iv Key words

One way of helping yourself to discover the main points of the lecture is to try to identify key words. During the course of most lectures, certain words or phrases recur which together sum up the lecturer's overall message. These will express the 'main ideas' and you will need to add some supporting details to them. While 'signposts' indicate the structure or shape of the lecture, the key words indicate the content - what it is about. After the lecture is over, at the 'review' stage mentioned later, you can highlight the key words and phrases in ways we suggest in the section on Mechanics.

When you come to read your notes later on, they will prompt your memory as to what the lecture was about. Looking for 'key words' and 'signposts' will help you listen attentively and help you to be selective in your note-taking. It will gradually help you to get an overview of the whole lecture, of the way the lecturer's mind works, and will begin to give you an insight into the ways of thinking in that particular discipline.

Stage 3: After the lecture

i Reviewing your notes

It is easy, especially with a crowded timetable, to put your notes away with a sense of satisfaction as soon as the lecture is over, and to forget about them until it is time to revise. But to make sure your notes are useful, you should check them over very soon after the lecture, either straight away or at least on the same day.

Are they legible? You may be able to read them on the same day, but what about later when you've forgotten the material?

Is the structure clear? If not, add headings, or underlinings, or indicate links (we will discuss layout of notes in the next section).

Most important, are you sure you know what your notes mean? If the structure isn't clear, maybe you have missed out something?

It is very useful to check your notes with a friend. Helping each other to clarify what was said will also help a great deal in remembering the lecture later, and in being able to make use of the ideas it contained. Research suggests that students who do not carry out a review of this kind may forget 75% of the material in a week and 98% in under three weeks. This means that by exam time, you have to start almost from scratch, with only your notes to help you.

So, with each lecture of a course, you should accumulate, step-by-step, a range of information, ideas and ways of approaching topics or problems. The process of review we have been suggesting is rather like that of building with blocks. Every now and again you have to stand back to survey the whole construction - look at how you have done and consider how it will eventually look. In the meantime, you are getting on with fitting each brick together.

ii Storing your notes

It is no use taking good notes if you waste time afterwards because you can't find them. Work out a simple 'storage' system for yourself and use it regularly, so that it is mechanical and you can save your time and effort for more important activities.

Loose-leaf files are easier to manage than exercise books because they can be rearranged as you build up a range of information; easiest of all, if you are affluent, or have affluent friends, is to store them on computer - but be sure you keep a back-up copy!

For instance, you may read about a particular topic at a different time from a lecture, and want to put the two sets of notes together. Most students use a loose-leaf file in college, for the day's notes, and keep a separate file at home for each subject. It is best to file away your notes as soon as possible after you have reviewed them, ideally on the same day as the lecture. Before you file away your notes, make sure the headings are clear, that they are dated and that the sources of your notes are clearly stated. These are obvious points, but can be easily forgotten at the time and will certainly be forgotten by a later date.

5
The Mechanics of Note-taking

The layout of notes

It is most important that notes are set out so that
you can easily understand them later on. To sort
out the mechanics of note-taking is not a trimming
process, but a means of making your notes more
effective in use. A visually clear and simple layout
will help you to 'read' the information easily later
on, and also will help you to keep the information
in your mind. A good layout scheme will include
leaving plenty of room on a page so that you can
take in information quickly when you look at it.
Remember that a page of notes should look quite
different from a page in a book. The key points
should jump out at you. It is also useful to save
plenty of space so that you can make additions or
alterations later. Leave a wide margin and space
between lines. This can also be useful to adding
your personal comments.

There are various ways of making the appearance
of your notes reflect the structure of the lecture.
Here are some suggestions you might like to
consider. You will not want to adopt all of them, all
together, but selectively used they can be very
useful.

i A numbering system

A numbering system will help you to divide up the
subject matter according to main points, less
important points, and supporting detail. Ideally,
you should devise your own system - and then try
to stick to it.

You could, for example, use the decimal system
which is very common in reports:

1   Main heading
1.1   First argument
1.1.1 Supporting arguments
1.1.2 Supporting arguments

You could also use a mixture of letters and numbers:

1, 2   Main headings (large subject division)
a, b   Sub-headings (sub-division of topic)

Another common combination is that of large and small Roman numerals:

I   Main section
i, ii   Sub-sections

You probably do already use some form of numbering systems - have a look at it, see if it's consistent, and consider how useful you have made it in ordering your material.

ii Indentation

You can indicate the importance of the topic by indenting from the margin; for instance, you could put your main heading next to the margin and indent your sub-headings.

iii A colour code

Underlining in general is a very useful and common method of indicating the more important lecture. But there are other categories of information you might need to indicate and here a colour code may be helpful. For instance, you sometimes take down a direct quotation from the lecture. Either you think the lecturer has said something particularly interesting or relevant, or s/he quotes from someone else. Make sure you are aware of the source of the quotation.

You could, for instance, box round the quotations in red, or underline the most important pieces of information in green, or underline your own ideas and comments on the lecture in blue. Again, design a code for yourself and then stick to it.

iv Diagrams, charts, tables

Express any information you can in diagrammatic or chart form. This is helpful firstly because it makes you analyse or organise your information, and also because, as we said earlier, it is easier to remember a visual image. These suggestions for layout may seem rather difficult to apply. If so, by looking at some past notes, you can see how easy it would be to add numbering, colour coding, underlining. If you have already used some of these techniques, consider whether you could add to them. Experiment to find which are the best techniques for you.

Organise your layout as much as you can during the lecture so that you can structure your notes as you take them. Some visual clues, however, can be added during the review stage when you have an overview of the lecture's structure, and time, for instance, to use several different colours.

The language of notes

It should now be clear that we don't think it is useful to try to write your notes in continuous prose using whole sentences. With certain kinds of lectures, it can be a good idea to try to write a complete summary of the whole lecture, but this would have to be done after the lecture, and would apply where you feel the need to reconstruct a whole argument.

We have discussed already the principle of selection in your notes. We are now looking at the need for compression in your note language. You simply don't have time during a lecture to write out full sentences. If your mind is actively processing the information you hear in a lecture it shouldn't be difficult to avoid writing complete sentences, because the way our minds work is closer to a briefer telegraphic language.

There are a number of common devices used to help to compress your notes. At the sentence level, leave out unnecessary words and use some linking signs:

=, eg., ie., (see list of abbreviations below).

At the word level, you can omit syllables, ie.,

gov't	**government**
hist	**historical**
electr	**electronic**

Sometimes, you can use initials instead of words eg., C of C (Chamber of Commerce). This will be easiest with words that occur frequently in your subject area so that your use of them becomes automatic. In addition, some people abbreviate common endings of words.

Work out yr. own abbrev. to suit subj. -
You should work out your own abbreviations to suit your subject matter.

These are some trick of the trade. Keep your own abbreviations simple and consistent, make sure you can recognise them later, and don't spend time in the lecture working out new ones. Here are some other abbreviations that can be very useful. Most people use a few favourites, ones that are most suitable for the type of subject matter and their own study purposes.

cf	**compare**
=	**equals**
eg.	**for example**
ie.	**that is**
ibid	**in same work**

Pattern notes

So far, we have been talking about notes set out in a linear way, with one idea following another over the page. But our minds don't necessarily work in this linear way, and sometimes neither does the structure of a lecture. A lecturer might easily go back to what he was talking about earlier, or jump from one idea to another. This can be rather confusing for the note-taker although it can be useful in showing links between ideas and in throwing up new ways of thinking about topics. Tony Buzan* has developed the idea of arranging notes in a pattern, rather than a linear sequence. It can be useful when you are making notes for an essay and sometimes, too, for a lecture.

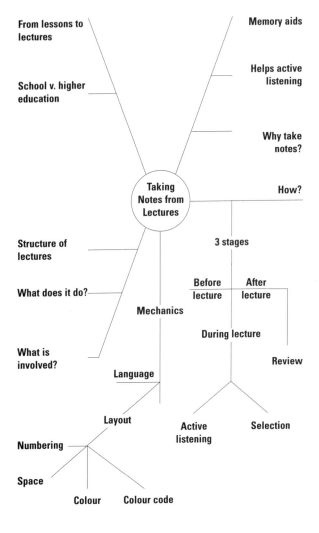

* Tony Buzan, *Use Your Head*, BBC, 1976

You place the main topic or title in the centre of the page, and link the main ideas around it. You can use lines to show links between ideas, which can show the structure of the lecture clearly. The visual pattern can help you to remember the information, and the use of simple phrases or single words saves you time and increases clarity.

If you have not tried this before, you could find it very useful for certain kinds of lectures. You could try it initially in two ways. Use it as a means of condensing and re-processing your notes while you are reviewing them. Or try it with a lecture you know will be fairly easy to understand. Alternatively, you could try taking your usual linear notes and, during the course of the lecture, build up your pattern notes as you go. Some students have found such diagrammatic note-taking methods have dramatically improved their studying. As we suggested before, it is also possible to express the structure of the lecture in other visual forms.

In this booklet, we have given you ideas about ways of approaching your lectures, to help you to learn from them more effectively. We have also suggested various techniques for taking notes from lectures, to help you to make notes which will be useful for your various study purposes. Think about your approach to listening to lectures and experiment with these different techniques to establish note-taking systems appropriate to your own study needs. Remember, too, that if you go to lectures prepared to be interested and to think about them, you will find it easier to take notes that will be useful to you later on.

Further Reading

Rowntree, D., Learn How to Study, Macdonalds, Chapter 7.

Buzan, T., Use Your Head, BBC, 1976 Chapters 5 & 6 (and video tapes, programmes 5 & 6).

Fisher Cassie, W. and Constantine, T., Student's Guide to Success, Macmillan, Chapter 4.

Brown, G., Learning from Lectures, Methuen.

Other Study Guides available from Blackwell's Bookshops:

Reading for Study

Are you reading effectively? For most students, reading is so automatic that you may not recognise it as a skill - and one that can be improved. Do you really get the best out of your books? Is your reading helping you as much as you would like? Do you wish you could read faster? This pocket-sized guide shows you how to improve your capacity to read for study, and how to adapt the way you read to the task in hand. Read it - you'd be surprised at what you could learn.

How to Write Essays

You may have all the facts at your fingertips and be brimming with theories and explanations, but are you doing yourself justice on paper? Giving help at every stage of the essay, from interpreting the question to the final follow-up, this handy pocket guide gives full, clear, concise guidance both for those who are tackling essays for the first time, and those who suspect that they could write them better.

Blackwell's Bookshops
50 Broad Street, Oxford OX1 3BQ

BY JORDANA TUSMAN

RUNNING PRESS
PHILADELPHIA · LONDON

CONTENTS

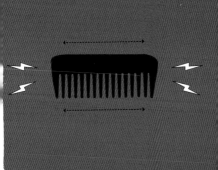

A Running Press® Miniature Edition™
© 2010 by Running Press

Library of Congress Control Number: 2009943425

ISBN 978-0-7624-3956-0

Photography, ©iStockphoto.com: April30 P6; R_Koopmans p8;
malerapaso p13; kaisersosa67 p19; SpellbindMe p25; blowbackphoto
p33; KevinDyer p39; MadCircles p45; saimnadir p53; Victorburnside
p61; NoDerog p67; jbreeves p73; creacart p79; bikec p89; dem10 p95;
GlobalP p103; pixhook p109; cutiebootiele p115; FotografiaBasica
p119; Eireanna p127; nazdravie p133; factoid p139; ooyoo p145;
kutaytanir p151; oktobernight p159

Running Press Book Publishers
2300 Chestnut Street
Philadelphia, PA 19103-4371

Visit us on the web!
www.runningpress.com

INTRO

The only thing more exciting than an open-bar night with all of your friends is impressing all of those friends with your amazing bar-trick skills. If those skills happen to involve flying bottle caps, disappearing coins, or doing cool things with lemons and toothpicks, so much the better.

Let's face it—we can't all be coordinated or cool enough to tie a cherry stem into a knot with our tongues. No matter who you are or what your boring story is, there is a wide assortment of inspiring tricks in this little book that will turn even the most foolish jokester

into a most sought-after bachelor or bachelorette. But it will take some careful study, practice, and concentration.

On the following pages you will find a selection of the most popular bar tricks, including tricks with matches, food, glasses, money, toothpicks, fire(!), and much more to amaze and astound your friends, strangers—and yes, hot dates—at the next classy dinner, crazy house party, or run-of-the-mill bar night you go out on.

Each bar trick lesson includes level of difficulty, components you'll need to perform the trick, and step-by-step instruction. And just like that old adage you learned back in kindergarten, practice truly makes perfect when it comes to performing a flawless bar trick—especially if you knocked back a few cocktails first.

Don't expect to perfect a bar trick by doing it just once or twice. Practice these tricks in front of a mirror or even a bunch of stuffed animals in the comfort of your own home until you've got the bar trick you want to master down pat. Then it's time to take your *Big Bad-Ass Bar Tricks* on the road and show everyone what you've got. Don't mess up! Cheers!

MATCHBOX HUT

LEVEL OF DIFFICULTY:

YOU'LL NEED:

1 MATCHBOX
2 MATCHSTICKS
1 LIGHTER
1 COIN

STEP 1: Keep your lighter hidden in your pocket for steps 1 through 3. Place the matchbox on a flat surface and stand one of the matchsticks red head up in the match tray. Close the tray so the matchstick can stand.

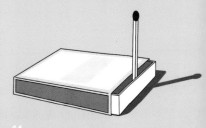

STEP 2: Place the coin on the matchbox. Place the second matchstick so its bottom is on the coin and the red head is leaning on the top of the other matchstick.

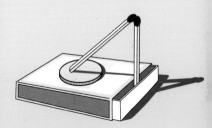

STEP 3: Challenge your opponent to remove the coin without touching the matchsticks or knocking them over.

STEP 4: When your opponent gives up, take out your hidden lighter and light the matchsticks' red heads. When the matchsticks start to burn, the match holding down the coin will start to bend upward and will stay connected to the other matchstick without falling.

STEP 5: You can then remove the coin from the matchbox without having ever touched the matchsticks or knocking them over.

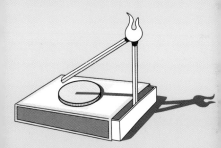

TIDAL WAVE

LEVEL OF DIFFICULTY:

YOU'LL NEED:

1 MATCHSTICK

1 LIGHTER

1 GLASS

1 LEMON OR LIME WEDGE

1 SAUCER FILLED WITH A
SPLASH OF WATER

STEP 1: Keep your lighter hidden in your pocket for steps 1 and 2. Tell your audience that you are going to transfer the water into the glass without pouring it in.

STEP 2: Place the lemon wedge on its side in the middle of the saucer and stick the matchstick (red head up) securely in the fruit, not the peel.

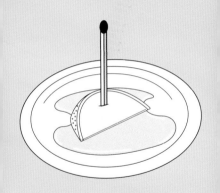

STEP 3: Reveal your lighter and use it to light the match in the fruit. Then, quickly place the glass over the burning fruit so the glass is touching the bottom of the saucer. This creates a vacuum of pressure and the water will be sucked into the glass.

NOTE: PRACTICE THIS TRICK A FEW TIMES BEFORE PERFORMING IT FOR AN AUDIENCE. YOU DON'T WANT TO LOOK LIKE A FOOL. IF YOU BECOME AN EXPERT AT THIS ONE, YOU CAN EVEN FLIP THE GLASS OVER AFTER STEP 3, MOUTH SIDE UP, AND ALL OF THE WATER FROM THE SAUCER WILL BE INSIDE THE GLASS.

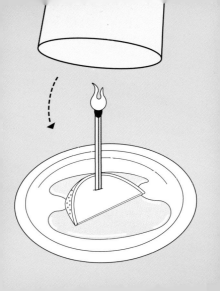

PAPER ROSE

LEVEL OF DIFFICULTY:

YOU'LL NEED:

2 NAPKINS

TAPE

STEP 1: This one will definitely impress the ladies. Take a napkin (colored ones make pretty roses) and completely unfold it.

STEP 2: Fold the napkin a couple of inches down and crease.

STEP 3: Roll the folded down side tightly, but start to roll a little looser as you get underway. When you get to the end of the napkin, you will have a pretty flower bud.

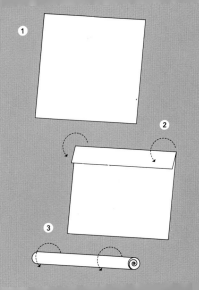

STEP 4: Pinch the bottom of the bud and roll the bottom of the napkin tightly to create a stem.

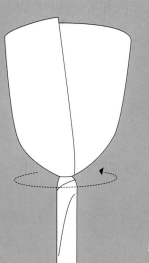

STEP 5: To create a leaf on the stem, tear a small corner off your second napkin. Attach the leaf to the stem with a small piece of tape. You can do this same step again farther down the stem if you want a second leaf.

STEP 6: Go crazy and make a full bouquet to truly impress.

> **NOTE:** THIS IS A FAIRLY UNCOMPLICATED WAY TO MAKE A PAPER ROSE. IF YOU WANT TO EXPLORE MORE INTRICATE ROSES, DO A GENERAL "PAPER NAPKIN ROSE" SEARCH ON THE INTERNET.

JUMPING PEPPER

LEVEL OF DIFFICULTY:

YOU'LL NEED:

- 1 SALT SHAKER
- 1 PEPPER SHAKER
- 1 PLASTIC COMB
- 1 BAR RAG
(or a cloth or t-shirt)

STEP 1: Keep the comb hidden in your pocket for steps 1 and 2. Pour a small amount of salt on a flat surface. Pour the same small amount of pepper on top of the salt.

STEP 2: Challenge an opponent to remove the pepper from the salt without touching either. Your opponent will look at you funny.

STEP 3: Pop the plastic comb out of your pocket and rub it hard against a bar rag to generate a good dose of static electricity.

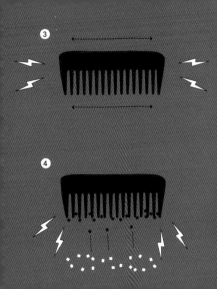

STEP 4: Hold the comb over the pepper. The pepper should separate itself from the salt and jump onto the comb. Neato!

NOTE: THIS TRICK WILL NOT WORK WITHOUT GENERATING ENOUGH STATIC ELECTRICITY, SO PRACTICE A FEW TIMES IN PRIVATE WITH THE RAG OR T-SHIRT BEFORE DOING THE TRICK, OR PREPARE TO BE HEAVILY LAUGHED AT.

FLYING CAP

LEVEL OF DIFFICULTY:

YOU'LL NEED:

1 UNOPENED BOTTLE
1 NAPKIN

STEP 1: Need to open a bottle and don't have a bottle opener? No problem. Challenge your opponent to open a beer bottle with a napkin. Unless he has superhuman strength, he will probably hurt his fingers if he prods the bottle cap too hard with his napkin.

STEP 2: When your opponent gives up, take the napkin and fold it from one corner to the opposite corner so it looks like a triangle. Then roll the bottom of the triangle very tightly to the top.

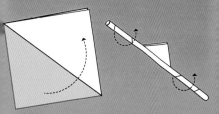

STEP 3: Your napkin should now look like a stick. Fold the napkin stick in half and place the top at the bottom of the bottle cap.

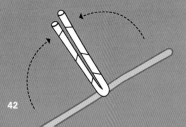

STEP 4: Hold the bottle down with one hand and use the other hand to pry the cap off with the napkin. With enough force, the cap will fly off the bottle.

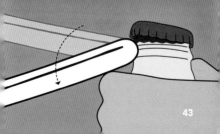

DISAPPEARING COIN

LEVEL OF DIFFICULTY:

YOU'LL NEED:

1 GLASS (a shot glass or smaller glass works best)

COLORED PAPER (the same color as the bar or table top)

1 NAPKIN

1 COIN **TAPE**

STEP 1: Before you perform the trick for your audience, go somewhere private. Cut out the small piece of paper (the same color of the flat surface you're going to perform the trick on), and tape it to the mouth of the glass. Be careful that your audience doesn't see the paper on the end of the glass as you put it on the flat surface.

STEP 2: Put the glass, mouth side down, on the flat surface.

Place a small coin like a penny or dime next to it. Tell your audience that you're going to make the penny disappear.

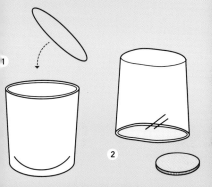

1

2

STEP 3: Place the napkin over the glass and coin. Then, move the glass on top of the coin. Wave your hands around on top and say some magical words or chant for effect. "You will disappear now, coin, disappear!" will do the trick.

STEP 4: Take off the napkin and show your audience that the coin has disappeared. After your crowd "oohs" and "ahhs," put the napkin back over the glass and remove the glass from over the coin, placing it once again next to the coin.

STEP 5: Remove the napkin once again and your audience will be amazed that the coin has reappeared. But don't linger—quickly snatch the glass and coin away and get rid of them. You don't want anyone examining your trick glass, or your amazing bar trick will be ruined.

OLIVE SNIFTER

LEVEL OF DIFFICULTY:

YOU'LL NEED:

1 OLIVE
1 BRANDY SNIFTER

STEP 1: Place an olive on a flat surface and a brandy snifter a few inches away from the olive.

STEP 2: Challenge your opponent to get the olive in the brandy snifter without touching the olive with any part of their body, scooping the olive into the snifter, or rolling the olive off the flat surface into the snifter.

STEP 3: When your opponent gives up, place the brandy snifter over the olive, mouth side down, and slowly rotate the snifter around the olive so that the olive starts to roll around the middle of the glass.

STEP 4: When the olive is comfortably rolling around the middle of the snifter, quickly flip the snifter into its upright position. The olive should now be inside the snifter.

BOTTLE PUSHER

LEVEL OF DIFFICULTY:

YOU'LL NEED:

1 DOLLAR BILL

1 EMPTY BEER BOTTLE

1 PEN OR PENCIL

STEP 1: Keep the pen hidden in your pocket for steps 1 and 2. Place a dollar bill on a flat surface and put a beer bottle upside down on the middle of the bill, mouth side down.

STEP 2: Challenge an opponent to remove the bill from under the bottle without touching the bottle or knocking it over.

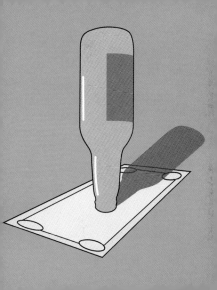

STEP 3: When your opponent gives up, put your pen at one end of the bill and slowly roll the bill around the pen toward the mouth of the bottle. Do this very slowly and carefully and you will eventually push the bottle off the bill.

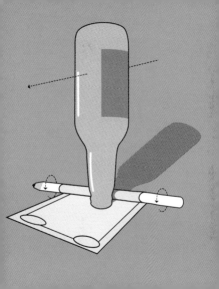

MATCHSTICK SPINNER

LEVEL OF DIFFICULTY:

YOU'LL NEED:

1 NICKEL

1 MATCHSTICK

1 PINT GLASS

1 COMB or A FEW STRAWS

STEP 1: This trick will wow your friends. Balance a nickel on its edge on a flat surface and then balance a matchstick on top of the nickel.

STEP 2: Put a pint glass upside down over the nickel and matchstick.

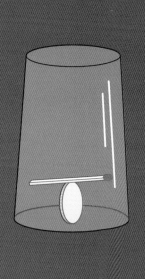

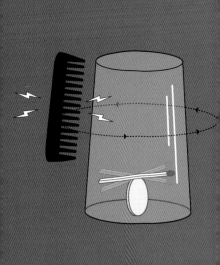

STEP 3: Rub a comb or a few straws roughly through your hair to create static electricity. Then, circle the comb or straws around the pint glass. Be careful not to touch the glass so the nickel doesn't fall. As the comb circles the glass, the matchstick will spin in circles on top of the nickel.

BILL SNATCH

LEVEL OF DIFFICULTY:

YOU'LL NEED:

2 EMPTY BEER BOTTLES

1 DOLLAR BILL

STEP 1: Place a beer bottle on a flat surface, a dollar bill on top of the bottle, and an upside down bottle on top of the bill. The bottles should be near the end of the bill rather than in the middle.

STEP 2: Challenge your opponent to remove the bill from the bottles without breaking any bottles or knocking them over. Your opponent will try to snatch the bill away from the bottles quickly, but he will be unsuccessful.

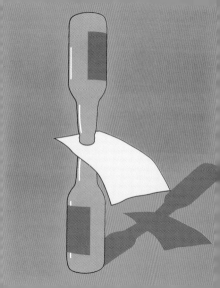

STEP 3: When your opponent gives up, hold the bill with one hand on the part of the bill that's farthest from the bottles.

STEP 4: With your free hand, bring your index finger down very fast on the bill. The spot to hit is between your hand holding the bill and the bottles. If done correctly, the bill should slap down perfectly and the bottles might wobble a little, but will not fall over.

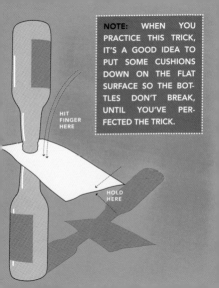

GLASS THROUGH TABLE

LEVEL OF DIFFICULTY:

YOU'LL NEED:

1 GLASS

1 COIN

A FEW NAPKINS

STEP 1: Sit down (this trick works best if you are seated) at the end of a table or flat surface. Your audience should be on the opposite side. Place a coin on the flat surface, put an upside down glass over the coin, and place the napkins over the glass, molding them down so that they take on the shape of the glass.

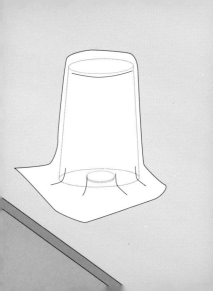

STEP 2: Tell your audience that you are going to make the glass and coin pass magically through the table.

STEP 3: Pretend you are concentrating hard and say "abracadabra" or something a bit more clever. Then, announce to your audience that the glass and coin have now passed through the table.

STEP 4: Lift up the glass and act astonished and irritated that the coin is still there. Repeat step 3, then lift up the glass again and act even angrier that the coin is still on the table. Repeat step 3 one more time, except this time, pick up the coin, yell at it, and exclaim that you have no idea why the coin isn't cooperating.

STEP 5: As you are distracting your audience with your crazy tantrum, use the hand that is holding the glass to slide it to the edge of the table and drop it into your lap. **DO NOT** drop the napkin. Be careful that the glass falls in your lap or else you will have broken glass and a ruined bar trick.

STEP 6: Slam the coin back on the table, put the glass-shaped napkins over it, and slam your fist down on it. Be sure to yell something like, "you stupid coin!" When the audience sees that the glass is nowhere in sight, announce that while the coin did not cooperate and pass through the table, at least the glass did!

STEP 7: Grab the glass from your lap and show it to the audience. You successfully made the glass pass through the table.

TOOTHPICK DOG

LEVEL OF DIFFICULTY:

YOU'LL NEED:

11 TOOTHPICKS
or **MATCHSTICKS**

1 TINY PAPER BALL

STEP 1: Put eleven toothpicks into the formation below to form a dog.

STEP 2: Put the tiny paper ball in the middle of the triangle, as seen below, for the dog's eye.

STEP 3: Ask your opponent to make the dog look the other way by only moving two toothpicks and the eye.

STEP 4: When your opponent gives up, move the two faded toothpicks and eye into the new formation (at right). The dog is now looking the other way.

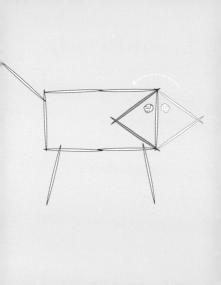

PSYCHIC COINS

LEVEL OF DIFFICULTY:

YOU'LL NEED:

1 ACCOMPLICE WITH A BEER

3 COINS

STEP 1: You will need an accomplice for this trick with a beer in his hand. He should be standing casually with your audience, careful not to look suspicious. Tell your audience that you are a psychic and you will be able to correctly guess which coin a victim of your choosing will touch when your back is turned.

STEP 2: Place three coins in a vertical line so there is one closest to you, one in the middle, and the third is closest to your audience.

STEP 3: Close your eyes, turn your back, and tell your victim to touch one of the coins so that everybody can see which one they have touched. Your accomplice should make sure he can see which coin the victim chose.

STEP 4: After the victim touches a coin, turn around and glance unsuspectingly at your accomplice. If the victim touched the coin closest to you, he should drink his beer a few times. If the victim touched the coin closest to him and the audience, he should hold the bottle up so it's level with his chest. If the coin in the middle was chosen, he should hold the beer down at his side.

STEP 5: After you study your accomplice, you can correctly guess the coin your victim chose and amaze your audience. You can do this trick a million times, as long as you and your accomplice do not act suspiciously.

INVASION OF THE MOUSE

LEVEL OF DIFFICULTY:

YOU'LL NEED:

1 LARGE, UNFOLDED NAPKIN

1 LEMON OR LIME

STEP 1: Unfold a large napkin and roll and twist the corners so they look like sticks.

STEP 2: Place the lemon under the napkin and push it across the bar top, flat surface, or floor and yell "mouse!" or anything else you can think of—spider, crab, bugs, rat, roach, or squirrel all work equally well. You could pretty much say anything as long as the creature is small enough. (It's crazy what people will actually think is under the napkin if you put an idea in their head.)

MOUSE!

STEP 3: When the lemon comes to a stop, feel free to take it one or two steps further and prod the napkin with your finger or a fork and yell "it's alive!"

BOXES

LEVEL OF DIFFICULTY:

YOU'LL NEED:

12 TOOTHPICKS or MATCHSTICKS

STEP 1: Set up twelve matches or toothpicks in the formation at right. Tell your opponent to make the four squares into three squares by only moving three matches. All of the matches have to be included in the formation of the boxes and there is no crossing or breaking of matches allowed.

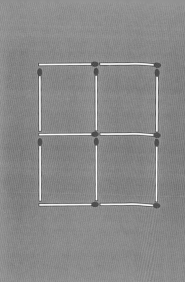

STEP 2: When your opponent gives up, move three matches (faded matchsticks) to their new positions, as shown in the formation at right.

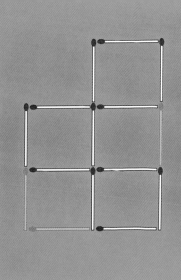

SIPPER

LEVEL OF DIFFICULTY:

YOU'LL NEED:

1 OPENED BEER BOTTLE
1 UNOPENED BEER BOTTLE

STEP 1: Challenge your opponent to drink beer from an unopened bottle.

STEP 2: When he or she looks at you like you're an idiot, and therefore forfeits, turn the bottle upside down, pour some beer from an opened bottle into the unopened bottle's recessed bottom, and sip up. Your opponent will still look at you like you're an idiot, but at least you proved them wrong!

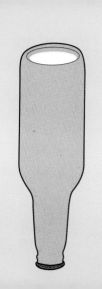

CORK BLOW

LEVEL OF DIFFICULTY:

YOU'LL NEED:

1 EMPTY BEER BOTTLE

**1 PLASTIC GROCERY-
STORE BAG**

1 CORK

STEP 1: Keep the plastic bag hidden for steps 1 and 2. Push the cork into the bottle. You might have to use a lot of force or a heavy object like the bottom of another empty beer bottle.

STEP 2: Once the cork is inside the bottle, challenge your opponent to remove the cork without breaking the bottle.

STEP 3: When your opponent gives up, get the hidden plastic bag and fold it lengthwise all the way to the end.

STEP 4: Place the bag inside the bottle, open side sticking out of the mouth of the bottle. Then blow into the bottle so the bag expands.

BLOW

STEP 5: Grip the end of the plastic peeking out of the bottle and slowly pull it out. The cork should come with it if you wiggle it just right.

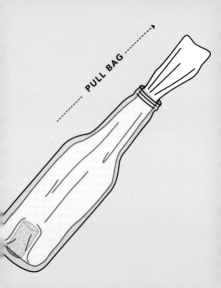

PULL BAG

TRAPPED COIN

LEVEL OF DIFFICULTY:

YOU'LL NEED:

1 GLASS

1 PENNY

4 QUARTERS

A TABLECLOTH ON THE TABLE

STEP 1: Stack two of the quarters. Then stack the other two quarters a few inches away from the first two. Put the penny in the middle of the two piles. Then place the glass upside down so the rim of the glass rests on top of the two quarter stacks. The penny will be inside.

STEP 2: Challenge your opponent to remove the penny without touching the glass or quarters or using any outside tools.

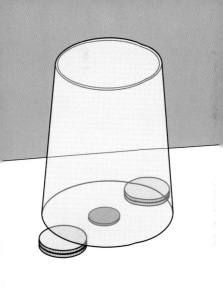

STEP 3: After your opponent gives up, it's your turn. The trick is the use of the tablecloth. Pinch a little piece of the table-cloth next to the outside of the glass, pull it up, and release.

STEP 4: Continue this motion until the penny "hops" its way out from under the glass. You can even pull it out once it's close enough to the edge of the glass.

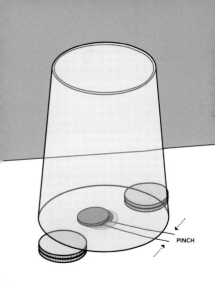

PINCH

T CAPS

LEVEL OF DIFFICULTY:

YOU'LL NEED:

6 BOTTLE CAPS

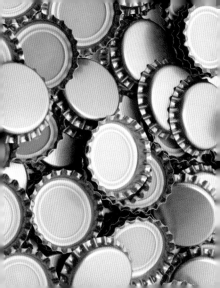

STEP 1: Place six bottle caps in a "T" shape by placing four bottle caps in a straight, vertical line and the other two caps on either side of the top cap.

STEP 2: Challenge your opponent to make two rows of four caps each by only moving one bottle cap.

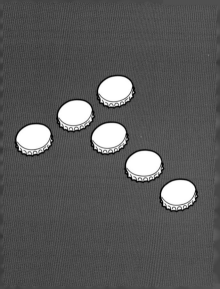

STEP 3: After your opponent messes up all the caps and fails miserably, put the caps back into the correct formation from step 1. Then take the bottle cap from the bottom of the "T" and put it on top of the cap in the middle. Be sure to exclaim "presto!" No one ever said the caps couldn't touch each other!

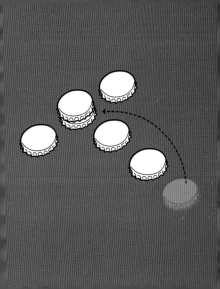

COIN PUZZLE

LEVEL OF DIFFICULTY:

YOU'LL NEED:

10 COINS

STEP 1: Place the coins into the formation at right.

STEP 2: Challenge your opponent to make the coins into an upside down triangle by moving only three of the coins. No new coins can be introduced to the triangle.

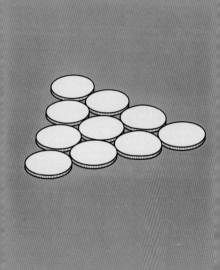

STEP 3: When your opponent gives up, move the three corner coins into their new positions so that they match the new formation, pictured at right. The triangle is now upside down.

COIN TOWER

LEVEL OF DIFFICULTY:

YOU'LL NEED:

SMALL NUMBER OF PENNIES (8 works best)

1 DIME

STEP 1: Stack the pennies into a tower on a hard, flat surface and place the dime on top.

STEP 2: Challenge your opponent to move the dime in the tower so that it's the second from the top. No coins in the tower can be touched except the dime, and one cannot simply find a penny that's not in the tower to place on top.

STEP 3: When your opponent gives up, find a penny that's not in the tower and slide it quickly at the tower so that the bottom penny gets pushed out from underneath.

STEP 4: Place the penny that got pushed out from underneath on top of the tower. The dime is now the second coin in the tower from the top.

FLYING PAPER CLIPS

LEVEL OF DIFFICULTY:

YOU'LL NEED:

1 DOLLAR BILL
2 PAPER CLIPS

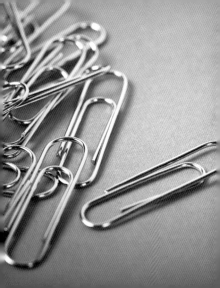

STEP 1: Tell your audience that without connecting the two paper clips together yourself, you will make them magically fly off the bill and connect together.

STEP 2: Fold one side of the bill to the middle and paper-clip the half to the center. Leave room at the end of the bill so that there is a small hole.

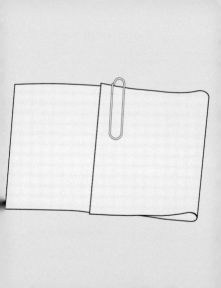

STEP 3: Then take the other side of the bill and fold it on top so that the edge hangs ever so slightly over the edge beneath it.

STEP 4: Paper-clip the edge of the bill to the inside of the small hole that you made in step 2. After this step, one paper clip will be on one side of the bill and the other paper clip will be on the other side. The paper clips hold the front and back parts of the bill to the two holes.

STEP 5: Gently pull the two sides of the bill so that the paper clips start to move closer and closer together.

STEP 6: When the paper clips are about to touch, quickly pull both sides of the bill. The paper clips will fly off the bill and be magically connected together when they land.

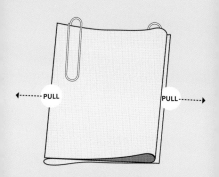

PULL

PULL

This book has been bound using
handcraft methods and Smyth-sewn
to ensure durability.

Designed & Illustrated by
Joshua McDonnell.

Written by
Jordana Tusman.

Edited by
Cindy De La Hoz.

The text was set in
Akzidenz, Avenir, and Block

BLOW